moments of hope

WALK THRU THE BIBLE®

Moments of Hope

40 Days of Encouragement for Women

TYNDALE
MOMENTUM®

A Tyndale nonfiction imprint

Visit Tyndale online at tyndale.com.

Visit Tyndale Momentum online at tyndalemomentum.com.

Tyndale, Tyndale's quill logo, *Tyndale Momentum*, and the Tyndale
Momentum logo are registered trademarks of Tyndale House Ministries.
Tyndale Momentum is a nonfiction imprint of Tyndale House Publishers,
Carol Stream, Illinois.

Walk Thru the Bible is a registered trademark of Walk Thru the Bible
Ministries, Inc.

Moments of Hope: 40 Days of Encouragement for Women

Adapted from *The One Year Walk with God Devotional: 365 Daily Bible
Readings to Transform Your Mind* by Chris Tiegreen, published in 2017
under ISBN 978-1-4143-3158-5.

For information about special discounts for bulk purchases, please
contact Tyndale House Publishers at csresponse@tyndale.com, or call
1-855-277-9400.

ISBN 978-1-4964-5752-3

Printed in the United States of America

30	29	28	27	26	25	24
7	6	5	4	3	2	1

Introduction

We are told in Romans 12:2 to be transformed by the renewing of our minds. As every Christian knows, that's a process. We did not come into this world with a clear perception about God and His Kingdom—or about our own selves, for that matter. We began with distorted views, and part of our task as Christians is to let God change our views to accurately reflect His character and His Kingdom. In other words, we need wisdom, encouragement, and hope that can be found only in Jesus.

That's what these readings are about. They are aimed at redirecting our thinking so we understand ourselves, our world, and our God accurately. They are designed to move us further along that path of having our minds renewed, our lives transformed, and our hope restored.

The focus in these devotionals is biblical wisdom, encouragement, and purpose so we can see how God's love, kindness, and dedication to us is found throughout the Scriptures. Every reading points to the truth God offers us freely and abundantly.

As you read these devotionals, remember that the Word of God expresses the mind and heart of God. His thoughts are available to you. Let these devotionals help you dig deeper into His hope for you. Let His Spirit change your thinking. Most of all, let your spirit be renewed and your life be transformed.

Be joyful in hope.
ROMANS 12:12

A Higher Mind

We have the mind of Christ.
1 CORINTHIANS 2:16

Hope In The Word

At first glance, Paul's claim is boastful. It would not go over well in our "politically correct" culture of today. It probably did not go over well in the Corinthian culture then, except within the church. There, it would have been a treasured truth and an amazing revelation.

So it is with us. It is almost unthinkable: The mind of the One through whom the entire universe was created, the fount of all wisdom, is available to us. We are not limited to human reasoning. We are not bound by the limitations of history's greatest thinkers, who, while often exceeding human standards of intelligence, have all fallen drastically short of discovering eternal truth by natural means. No, we have a supernatural access to ultimate reality from an eternal perspective. We know the direction of history and where it is leading; we know how to escape this fallen world; and we know who holds all power in the palm of His right hand. This vast, incomprehensible treasure is ours—if we will accept it.

That's our problem. We often resort to lesser means of wisdom because we're unaware that the mind of Christ is accessible, or we're unable to believe such an extravagant promise. But if we can't believe it, we can't have it. The mind of Christ is ours through the Spirit of God, who comes to us only through faith. The Spirit searches the deep things of God (1 Corinthians 2:10) and reveals them to His people. Such things are foolish to the world, but they are truth nonetheless—truth that we can know and base our lives on.

Hope In Deed

You have your own mind. You also have Christ's. Which would you rather depend on? Begin each day by disavowing your own wisdom. We must acknowledge that we do not have the understanding to make the decisions we will face each day. We do not know all the details or future implications of any decision. But God does, and He makes His wisdom available. Acknowledge your utter dependence on the mind of Christ, ask for His wisdom, and believe.

The truly wise are those
whose souls are in Christ.
ST. AMBROSE

In Defense of Truth

The LORD detests lying lips, but he
delights in people who are trustworthy.
PROVERBS 12:22

Hope In The Word

Dishonesty is epidemic in our culture. Court
records, academic surveys, and common observation
confirm it. Truth and integrity are expendable in our
society.

Why do people lie? Or, to put it more subtly and
inclusively, why do virtually all of us sometimes try

to create an impression that isn't entirely accurate? The reasons are many and varied. They include a desire to stay out of trouble, a drive to get ahead, and an obsession about our image. In any case, a person's dishonesty indicates a lack of trust in God for the consequences of integrity. When we lie—even in a seemingly insignificant way—it is because we are avoiding the results of not lying. We take matters into our own hands because we're afraid of what will happen if we tell the truth. We do not trust God to honor our integrity.

But our God is a God of integrity. It is in His character. He never lies, and He is not silent when the truth needs to be revealed. It is His nature to be absolutely reliable. There is no hint of pretense in Him. He is who He says He is, He does what He says He will do, and He honors those who follow His lead. Always.

Hope In Deed

This is both comforting and convicting. It is comforting because we know that God's promises in His Word are reliable. When He inspires prophecy, it is accurate. When He promises blessing, it will come. When He says He will defend His people, He will. We can read His Word with unwavering assurance that it is pure truth with no fine print hidden away from our trusting eyes.

But the purity of God's character is also convicting. We know that though we are called to be like Him, our integrity falls short of His. He is shaping us to reflect His glory, but when we give a false impression, we interfere with His work.

Trust God with the truth. Tell it and display His integrity. Know that He will always defend truth—and those who tell it.

Where truth is, there is God.
MIGUEL DE CERVANTES

Perfect Timing

I waited patiently for the LORD; he
turned to me and heard my cry.
PSALM 40:1

Hope In The Word

Patience is one of the hardest virtues for us to understand. We pray to an omnipotent God. We know He is able to help us at any moment. We know that He who defines Himself as "love" and gave His Son for us is not reluctant to help us. So when we ask such a God to intervene in our circumstances, why is there so often a delay?

Nowhere in the Bible does God promise us instant answers to our prayers. His promises for answered prayer are amazing and reassuring, but none of them includes a timetable. He only assures us that He is never too late. Yet in our impatience, we don't want an answer that is simply "not too late." We want an answer now. We have needs, and we do not understand why those needs must be prolonged.

But God has His reasons. Perhaps our needs are being prolonged because they are accomplishing something in us that nothing else will. Perhaps they are being prolonged because God is doing a necessary work in the life of someone else who is involved in our situation. Perhaps He is teaching us about prayer or perfecting our faith. Maybe He is even letting us identify with Jesus in the fellowship of His sufferings—it is, after all, His overarching purpose to conform us to the image of Christ. How can we be conformed if we have no identification with His pain?

Hope In Deed

Sometimes God will make clear that our answer is delayed because the delay will further His work in our own hearts or in another area. Sometimes

He gives us no reason at all. The Christian's wise response, in either case, is to know that if we are waiting on God, there must be a very good reason. And if we wait in faith and expectancy, the wait will be amply rewarded. His timing is always perfect.

Simply wait upon Him. So doing, we shall be directed, supplied, protected, corrected, and rewarded.

VANCE HAVNER

A Heart and a Song

My heart, O God, is steadfast, my heart
is steadfast; I will sing and make music.
PSALM 57:7

Hope In The Word

Reading the Psalms, one gets the impression that life
for its writers, especially David, was one tumultu-
ous episode after another. There are psalms of praise
and joy, of grief and defeat, of deep meditation
and inspiring victory. But regardless of the focus of
each psalm, it is hard not to notice that many of

them—most, in fact—are written in the context of crisis (see 57:1, for example). Cries to God come out of the crucible, and God's response comes into it.

One thing God looks for when we are in the crucible is a steadfast heart—a heart that will not, under any circumstances, fall away. No matter what uproar is going on around us, no matter how much pressure is applied, God will wait to answer us until it is clear to Him, to us, and to those who observe us, that our heart is resolutely fixed on Him. And more than just steadfastness of hope is required; it is a steadfastness of worship, too. The heart that learns to make music in its darkest moments is the heart that is delivered.

The deliverance usually comes twice. First, a worshipful heart has risen above oppressive circumstances, even when the circumstances remain. It is an inward liberation that can find deep joy regardless of what's happening on the outside. But a resolved, singing heart then finds deliverance in a God who responds. He frequently invades circumstances and scatters our enemies, sometimes dramatically. The wait may be long, but the victory is sure. God does not remain silent in His love when we do not remain silent in our worship.

Hope In Deed

When circumstances oppress, the battle rages, and the heat of the crucible rises, where is your heart? Is it steadfast in its worship? Does it sing of the God who reigns above every cloud? If so, expect deliverance. Expect it within and without. You can sing your song of victory before victory even comes. In the most important sense, it already has.

Streams of mercy, never ceasing,
call for songs of loudest praise.
ROBERT ROBINSON

Representing Jesus

Whatever you do, work at it with
all your heart, as working for the
Lord, not for human masters.
COLOSSIANS 3:23

Hope In The Word

We see our lives in terms of activity and achievement.
We interpret our success in terms of what we've
accomplished. So it only makes sense that when we
work, we define its quality by externals—what we've
done, whom we've done it for, and what results it will
have.

God has His eye on other criteria. He sees our lives in terms of fruit, which may include activities and achievements but encompasses so much more. Fruit involves those qualities the Holy Spirit cultivates in us—love, joy, peace, patience, kindness, goodness, faithfulness, gentleness, and self-control (Galatians 5:22-23). So when God sees us at work, He is more interested in how the work is being done than in what it accomplishes. He looks at motives and attitudes. Most of all, He looks to see if our motivation is derived from Him or if He is peripheral to what we do. And if He is peripheral, He is grieved.

Ultimately, every inch of our lives is God's, even our work. If He wants to be Lord of our thoughts and our relationships, He clearly would also want to be Lord of our employment, or whatever vocation occupies our time. We do not cease being His disciples when we punch a time clock. If He is truly our Lord, then everything we do is for Him.

Hope In Deed

Do you work for an employer? Perhaps so, but the impression you make on him or her is entirely God's business. He is zealous for the reputation of His name. If you have claimed His name, He is therefore zealous for your reputation. Your character and His go hand in hand. If other people—believers and nonbelievers alike—observe godly qualities in you, then God is glorified. If they don't, He isn't. We literally represent Jesus wherever we are, including the workplace. Represent Him with all your heart.

**A dairy maid can milk cows
to the glory of God.**
MARTIN LUTHER

New Clothes

> You were taught, with regard to your
> former way of life, to put off your old
> self . . . and to put on the new self.
> EPHESIANS 4:22, 24

Hope In The Word

Living the Christian life should become as natural
to us as changing clothes. We take off the old and
we put on the new. The old may have been comfort-
able, but it is dirty and horribly out of fashion in our
new kingdom. The new is the permanent style of the
Kingdom of Heaven, and it will cause us to resemble

God increasingly. Our responsibility is to continually shed what is no longer appropriate and put on the clothes we have been given.

But many of us walk an unwise path. We claim citizenship in the new kingdom but continue to wear the fashions of the old. In trying to fit in everywhere, we find that we fit in nowhere. We may blend into the old kingdom, but we no longer have proper ID there. We have the proper ID for the new kingdom, but we're slow to fit in. Either way, it's an awkward situation to be in.

What is our reluctance? Why do we hesitate to put on our new clothes? Because we know we will experience rejection, and no one likes rejection. But rejection will come to everyone, either from the world or from the Kingdom of Heaven. The question is not whether we can avoid it, but whose we most want to avoid. Wisdom calls for a choice. Trying to dress for both kingdoms is not a viable option.

Hope In Deed

Are you reluctant to place both feet firmly in the Kingdom of God? Do you try to hang on to remnants of your former citizenship? Let them go. Shed them like an old set of ragged clothes. The way to settle into your new kingdom and advance in it is to be reclothed. It's a daily process. We deny deceitful desires (Ephesians 4:22) and saturate ourselves in a new attitude (4:23). We become like God in righteousness and holiness (4:24). There is no greater wisdom than this.

We cannot help conforming ourselves to what we love.
ST. FRANCIS DE SALES

Count Yourself

**Count yourselves dead to sin but
alive to God in Christ Jesus.**
ROMANS 6:11

Hope In The Word

Nowhere is there a clearer connection between
wisdom—the renewed mind that God gives us in
Christ—and our life in the Spirit than in this verse.
Our encounter with life in Christ, according to Paul,
stems from what we *know* to be true. The truth of
our life is a matter of what Jesus did for us on the

Cross and the third day; our experience of it is a matter of our mental grasp of this truth. We are to count ourselves dead but also alive. Other translations also make it an issue of our thought-life. We are to consider, to reckon, to count on the truth: We died with Jesus and we are raised with Him.

Many Christians miss out on experiencing the victorious, joy-filled life, not because they aren't in fact crucified and raised in Jesus, but because they don't know it. Perhaps it is only a theological belief or a matter of creed. Perhaps it is misunderstood as something to strive for rather than to accept. Perhaps it is seen as a future possibility rather than an established position. None of that is enough. A Christian will really experience the joy and power and victory of the Christian life when he or she believes its foundation: We were crucified with Jesus, and now we are raised in His life. And it must be more than belief; we must know it, count on it, cling to it as a rock-solid event as certain as the day we graduated, got married, or signed a contract.

Hope In Deed

Too many Christians are trying to make the Christian experience true for them. They have put the cart before the horse. Experience doesn't lead to truth; truth leads to experience. Instead of praying for the resurrected life, accept it and live it. Instead of hoping you will die to sin, count on the fact that you already have. Our struggles are often only a product of how we see ourselves. If we see ourselves as sinners trying to be better Christians, that is how we'll live. If we see ourselves as sinners who were buried with Christ and raised to new life, that too is how we'll live. Romans 6:11 tells us what to see. Count on it, and watch your experience line up with truth.

You do not need to wait . . . before beginning to live eternally.
JAMES S. STEWART

A Personal Walk

Whoever fears the LORD walks
uprightly, but those who despise
him are devious in their ways.
PROVERBS 14:2

Hope In The Word

In our individualistic culture, we tend to think that
our behavior is our own domain. "It's my life," "It's
my body," "It's nobody's business but my own," are
all common declarations of independence that most
of us have heard—or even said—often. We see ourselves as isolated actors on a crowded stage. People
do their own thing.

That was the philosophy in the period of the judges too. "Everyone did as they saw fit" (Judges 21:25). They used their own standards of morality not only because they had no king, but also because they disregarded God. In our era of tolerance, we are immersed in a philosophy of "to each his own." Anyone claiming an absolute standard of behavior is sure to hear the mantra of the age: "As long as it's not hurting anyone else, it doesn't matter what a person does." God has a direct response: It matters.

Why does it matter? Because those who are upright in heart and behavior show a respect for God and His ways. Those who are not—who are devious in their plans and destructive in their ways—show that they couldn't care less that God exists. His standards are irrelevant to them. Ideas, behaviors, and lifestyles are not just personal decisions affecting only ourselves; they are personal statements about the God who created us. What we think and what we do says a lot about the One we serve.

Hope In Deed

Have you made that connection between your lifestyle and your opinion of God? The two are intimately linked. Those who fear God with respect and awe will reflect it in their lives. Those who don't believe God exists—or don't care that He does—will also reflect that in their lives.

In an independent age, that's a foreign thought. We who believe the Word can no longer say, "My life is my business." Our lives are statements of who He is. Consider your thoughts, your words, and your actions well. Understand the statement you are making.

Only he who believes is obedient, and only he who is obedient believes.
DIETRICH BONHOEFFER

Gold That Remains

When he has tested me,
I will come forth as gold.
JOB 23:10

Hope In The Word

Few of us would have the confidence Job did. We might rather assume that when God has tested us in the same manner that gold is refined, many impurities will be consumed. Eventually, perhaps, we will come forth as gold, but not immediately. Sin runs too deep and the refining takes so excruciatingly long.

Perhaps it is overconfidence that leads Job to say such a thing, or perhaps he really was that much more righteous than the rest of us. Either way, whether he is right about himself or not, he has hit on a foundational spiritual principle: God tries His servants, and the intended result is pure gold.

Just as the Cross of Jesus revealed the character of God within Him, so does the fire of trial reveal the character of God within us. Are we patient? We and the world will only know it if our patience is tested. Are we loving? It will not be seen until we are confronted with hatred. Are we full of faith? There's no evidence until circumstances dictate against it. Every fruit of the Spirit is latent within us until its antithesis appears. Superficial joy and real joy look exactly the same until the storm comes and blows one of them away. Peace isn't really peace unless it can survive when attacked. And deeper still: Your life in the Spirit isn't life at all if it melts away when death threatens.

Hope In Deed

We want all the fruits of the Spirit and all of the blessings of Christlikeness, but we rarely realize the cost. Nothing God gives us is proven genuine until it is assaulted by the troubles of this world and the wiles of the enemy. It is the only way God reveals Himself through His saints. It is the only way the authentic is distinguished from the superficial. It is the only way to come forth as gold.

Are you running from tests? Don't. Stand firm in them. Let God do His purifying work. Get ready to shine.

In shunning a trial, we are
seeking to avoid a blessing.
CHARLES SPURGEON

The Priority to Pursue

Let love and faithfulness never leave you;
bind them around your neck,
write them on the tablet of your heart.
PROVERBS 3:3

Hope In The Word

Solomon's words would have had familiar connotations for a faithful Jew. In Deuteronomy 6, a landmark chapter in Old Testament theology, God told the Israelites first to love Him with all their heart, soul, and strength. Then He told them to take the words of the Law, divinely inscribed on tablets of

stone, and inscribe them into the fabric of their souls.
Let them be always on your hearts, He commanded.
Work them into your children's hearts. Talk about
them always. Tie them as symbols on your hands
and foreheads. Never be away from them (see
Deuteronomy 6:4-9).

The interesting connection between
Deuteronomy and Proverbs is that the Law is
defined as "love and faithfulness." It is also interesting that Deuteronomy is specific in where our
love and faithfulness are first to be directed: toward
God. The foremost element of a believer's life is
not obedience, not service, and not doctrine. These
are important—indispensable, in fact. But they
are not the priority. Love is. A passionate, vital, all-
encompassing love that reaches to the depths of our
being. When that is there, the rest is easy.

Hope In Deed

Do you consider your heart to be a tablet? What is
written on it? Do you realize that some things can be
erased by the power of God and others inscribed by
that same power? It requires your full cooperation,
but the junk that we've inscribed there—through
all of the media and entertainment we absorb,
the relationships we've had, the information we

consume—can be rewritten. It can be replaced with love and faithfulness. In fact, it *must* be replaced with love and faithfulness if we are to learn the mind of our God at all. This is who He is, and He insists that we become like Him. Love and faithfulness define Him. Do they define you? Let them saturate your heart.

Put everything you have into the
care of your heart, for it determines
what your life amounts to.
DALLAS WILLARD

A Way to Give Honor

Honor the LORD with your wealth.
PROVERBS 3:9

Hope In The Word

We're often not conscious of the statements we
make, but they are more numerous than we think.
We aren't aware of them because most are not verbal.
They are revelations of the heart, spoken by our
choices. As is often said, actions speak louder than
words.

Consider, for example, what we are saying when we have no money for God's ministry but enough to pay the cable bill. Or when we see the starving and wish we could help—and then waste money on soft drinks with no nutritional value. Why does thirty dollars a month to save a child seem like so much, and thirty dollars for a steak dinner for two seem like such a bargain? What do our choices say of God? Not much. They say more about our values. They reveal what's in our heart.

God is no enemy of entertainment and taste buds. But He is an enemy of idols, and our choices reveal what they are. We deceive ourselves often—our enormous capacity for doing so came with the Fall. It's amazing how much we can't afford to do for God's Kingdom—the budget is always tight, right? Meanwhile, the vacations we really want to take are usually taken. The meals we really want to eat are usually eaten. The make and model we want to drive is usually in our driveway. We more comfortably delay God's gratification than our own.

Hope In Deed

We need to snap out of our unconsciousness. Many of our idols have become automatic to us. We don't see them as intentional choices that reveal the treasures of our heart. But deep down we know: If we loved God with all of our being, if we treasured His Kingdom above all else, He would see more of our treasure given for His use.

Why is this so important? Does God have insufficient funds? Probably not. The Owner of all isn't short of cash when He really wants to accomplish something. He wants more than cash. He wants us to value faith, the currency of His Kingdom, over the currency of this world. More than that, He wants us. He wants our choices to reflect an intense, unbridled love. He wants them to honor Him.

Get all you can, save all you can, and give all you can.
JOHN WESLEY

A Heart at Peace

A heart at peace gives life to the body.
PROVERBS 14:30

Hope In The Word

The relationship between the spirit and the body is deeper than we might think. Not all physical infirmity is a product of spiritual turmoil, but much of it is. When God is on the periphery of our lives, our bodies can't stand the void. Ask anyone who has heart trouble. Stress is often a big part of it. And stress is the result of a too-distant God.

Peace has prerequisites. One of them is a surrender of all the self's attempts to earn God's approval. Instead, we are to understand that God approves of Jesus and we are related to Jesus by faith. Another is an inspired ability to trust God, even when circumstances seem to dictate against trust. But there is one often assumed prerequisite to peace that is a decidedly misguided assumption. Peace is *not* dependent on circumstances. Not real peace, anyway. The real peace that comes from God is available in spite of circumstances. And it is often revealed *only* in the difficult times. We never know the truth of our relationship with God until it is burned in the fire. Does it remain? Then it is gold; it is true. Or does it collapse? Then it was combustible from the very beginning, worth nothing at all. Peace from God must be tested. If it isn't, we never know whether it's genuine.

Hope In Deed

We human beings are a strange mixture of mind, body, and spirit. We like to think of these as separable entities, but they are not. They interrelate at levels we can scarcely understand. Sin has physical effects. Mental stress has physical effects. And a heart at peace gives life.

Whatever you are going through—and it is a safe assumption that we are always going through something—it is not to affect your peace. God is above your circumstances, and He is greater than your sin. Bring it all to Him—your sin, your trials, your everything. Bind yourself to the things that really matter and the One who can govern them. And rest. Be at peace and be well.

**Peace rules the day when
Christ rules the mind.**
ANONYMOUS

Real Refuge

The LORD helps them and delivers
them; he delivers them from the
wicked and saves them, because
they take refuge in him.

PSALM 37:40

Hope In The Word

What does it mean to take refuge in God? It means
to have faith that what He says is true; He will deliver
those who call on Him. It means to appeal to Him
in times of trouble; prayer is a powerful resource.
But most of all, it means that we decide not to take
refuge in ourselves, in others, in worldly wisdom,

or in human strategies. We take refuge in Him, *and Him alone*.

What do you do when you're in trouble? If you're like most believers, you figure out a strategy and ask God to bless it. In His mercy, He may. But He calls us to a better way. When God tells us He is our refuge, He asks us to forsake our former allegiance to other sources of protection. Are you sick? First acknowledge that no medical treatment will work unless God is the Healer behind it. Are you in conflict with someone else? First acknowledge that no words of yours will change another's heart unless God is the agent of change. Are you in financial distress? First acknowledge that no amount of income will help unless God is the source. And having acknowledged all of this, look to Him constantly. Follow His instructions for action, but know first that your action is God-directed and not a futile means of self-help.

God is a Deliverer for those who recognize how helpless and vulnerable they are. He is not a Deliverer for those who try to add Him to their own self-effort.

Hope In Deed

"God helps those who help themselves" is a catchy saying, but it is not biblical. Rather, God helps those who know how helpless they are and who appeal to Him—on His terms—for deliverance. That's not quite as catchy, but it's true. Those who want God to be their stronghold in times of trouble must actually *depend* on God as their stronghold. The deliverance is His, and His alone.

Dear Lord, although I am sure of my position, I am unable to sustain it without you. Help me or I am lost.
MARTIN LUTHER

Day 14

Our Highest Purpose

God created mankind in his own image,
in the image of God he created them;
male and female he created them.

GENESIS 1:27

Hope In The Word

No one can live wisely and with purpose without
realizing where we came from, where we are going,
and why it all came about in the first place. That is
the foundation for everything. If we don't understand that, we don't understand the gospel and we
don't have the context to make daily decisions that

will align with God's plan. We must know: We are created from Him, for Him, and in His likeness.

It's a remarkable truth. We were meant to be the image of God, and though the image was shattered in the Fall, God's original intention lives on. He was not surprised by the Fall, and His plan included fashioning a people who would reflect His glory. He still means for us to bear His image. That's why He has put His Spirit in the heart of sinful but redeemed mankind—these earthen vessels that we are.

Humanity *will* bear His image. He *will* be seen in this creation. Never mind that His image-bearers once forfeited that privilege. Even before we lost it, He had determined to recraft it in us. He bears His image in us Himself.

Hope In Deed

We get caught up in jobs, mortgages, family business, relationships, and pastimes, trying to find some sense of fulfillment in all of them. It's easy to get distracted that way. But we have a higher calling lying underneath it all. *We are made to be like Him!* That's the point of it all. That was the purpose of our first parents, and that is the purpose of our redemption. Adam and Eve were modeled after Him; but we are even inhabited by Him. We are daily being conformed to the image of God in Christ (2 Corinthians 3:18).

Do you live with that awareness? Are your mundane, daily decisions made with that in mind? Meditate on this amazing truth daily and let it guide your life. Whatever your other desires, there is no higher calling than this. It's what we were made for.

Common sense suits itself to the ways of the world. Wisdom tries to conform to the ways of heaven.
JOSEPH JOUBERT

Dreamers and Doers

Those who work their land will
have abundant food, but those who
chase fantasies have no sense.
PROVERBS 12:11

Hope In The Word

Dreams are wonderful. God gives us dreaming hearts
because He wants us to accomplish things. In the
heart that dreams, God can plant visions of wide-
spread, effective ministries, of preaching the gospel
and helping the poor, of finding innovative ways
to build the Kingdom of Heaven. He can inspire

millions and set the course of nations. Dreams are the beginning of all good accomplishments.

The problem with dreams is that they are just the beginning. In themselves, they don't accomplish anything. They may be the fuel that feeds the fire, but they aren't its substance. A life full of fantasies, no matter how worthy the fantasies, is futile if no action ever springs forth from its ambitions. Though God plants dreams in our hearts, He does not simply leave them there. He expects the keepers of the land to till the soil, water the seeds, and cultivate their growth. God wants our visions to have a plan of action.

Jesus told a parable that illustrated that principle. A man had two sons. One of them said he would work in the vineyard but never did. The other said he wouldn't but eventually did anyway. Which one did Jesus praise? The doer, not the dreamer (Matthew 21:28-32).

Hope In Deed

Do you have big plans? Do you have a vision you're convinced God has given you? If so, what are your plans? God is expecting you to take the visions He has given you and move them forward. Write the steps down. Then take them. Don't let your dreams become faint memories of the night.

Are you unsure of your dreams? Still trying to determine whether they are self-ordained or God-given? Then ask God specifically to encourage the ones that are also His dreams for you. But once you know the difference, don't let them sit. Ask for His timing. Ask for His wisdom. And act on His promises.

Dreams grow holy put into action.
ADELAIDE PROCTOR

The Battle Within

Give me an undivided heart,
that I may fear your name.
PSALM 86:11

Hope In The Word

Is there a Christian alive who has not struggled with a dual nature? Probably not. We who are gloriously born of the Holy Spirit of God are also genetically confirmed, card-carrying descendants of Adam. The Spirit enables us to live godly lives, but our tendency to do so is sporadic. While our spirit is often willing, the flesh remains weak. The Jekyll-and-Hyde syndrome may be common to all mankind, but it is especially common to the redeemed. Two natures in one body can make for an exhausting struggle. Are you exhausted yet? Don't think you are alone. You're not.

The burden of the divided heart is common in Scripture. It is the burden of which Paul wrote in Romans 7—"I have the desire to do what is good, but I cannot carry it out" (verse 18). It is the same contradiction Peter felt, claiming one evening that he could never forsake his Lord, then denying Him three times the same dark night. Every one of us has—at least occasionally—known the anguish of a divided soul.

A false solution to the problem has become epidemic. It is to resign oneself to the lower of the two natures, forfeiting the call to be holy as God is holy (1 Peter 1:15). Mistakenly calling true holiness "legalism," we can become far too accepting of our corruption. We sometimes even embrace it. We give up the battle and let the old nature win.

Hope In Deed

There is a wiser way, and it is the work of God's Spirit, not of ourselves. We will never be completely delivered from the fight until we are in heaven, but victory is possible. Paul said so (Romans 7:24-25), and after Pentecost, Peter would agree. God answers the prayer of the psalmist; an undivided heart is possible. *Ask for it daily!* Be aware of all that would compete for the throne of God in your heart. Take your attention off of it, whatever it is, and put it on the breathtaking beauty of God. Be captivated by Him alone. If your heart is immersed in Him, sin will have no room to thrive.

No one ever lost out by excessive devotion to Christ.
H. A. IRONSIDE

Unshakable

When calamity comes, the wicked
are brought down, but even in death
the righteous seek refuge in God.
PROVERBS 14:32

Hope In The Word

How do you react in a crisis? Or, to ask an even
more revealing question, how do you react in the
minor irritations of everyday life? The answer is not
a matter of what you say you believe. It's a matter
of your familiarity, even intimacy, with your Father.
As much as we say that He is trustworthy and true,

our tower of strength and our shield, those are only words until they are tested. And in this world, they are tested often.

Have you ever known Christians who believe the right things about God but who panic at every difficulty? It's hard to believe that someone's belief in the sovereignty and faithfulness of God are more than skin deep when his panic sets in. The truth of our relationship with God comes out when the heat is on. We discover whether we really trust Him or not when we're put in a position of having to trust Him. A belief in God's providence means little until one lacks essentials, and a belief in God's strength means little until one is completely helpless. Then the truth comes out.

Those who have not put their trust in the Refuge, who ignore Him and go their own way, are wicked, according to the Bible. That may seem harsh, but that's the true assessment of the human rebellion. And those who do not really trust Him will be brought down by every calamity. Those who do trust Him can't be brought down by anything—even death.

Hope In Deed

So where do you stand? Do you have a shallow belief in God's faithfulness, applying His promises to others' situations but not to your own? We are called to live in a different dimension than we once lived in. We must *know* who our Fortress is. We are not to become strong; we are to find our strength in Him. We must let His peace speak louder to us than our trials do. God stands firm when everything else moves. Can you?

As sure as God puts His children
in the furnace, He will be in
the furnace with them.
CHARLES SPURGEON

Radical Transformation

Just as he who called you is holy, so
be holy in all you do; for it is written:
"Be holy, because I am holy."
1 PETER 1:15-16

Hope In The Word

Our familiarity with the gospel often dulls us to
history's most spectacular truth: Human beings can
have a relationship with the unimaginably awesome
God. Perhaps having heard this so many times has
led us to take it for granted, but it's Scripture's most
startling claim and a truly overwhelming thought for
anyone who will let it sink in.

What makes this possible? The cleansing sacrifice of Jesus removes our impurity and makes us pure. But this is the legal side of the issue. What makes an ongoing, intimate relationship with the Almighty a practical reality? Holiness. The process of becoming like Him. Those among us who need impressive theological terms to validate a doctrine call it "sanctification." If the substitutionary sacrifice of Jesus is the basis for our relationship with God, our sanctification is its practical application. We cannot know Him well without it.

That's what makes this truth of a relationship with God so startling. When we first learn who He is, we come face-to-face with an overwhelming obstacle: A thoroughly sinful man cannot get along with a perfectly holy God without one of them having a radical change of character, and we know God isn't going to be the one to change. He can't. It must be us.

Hope In Deed

Far too many Christians are content with the legal basis of their salvation without taking much thought to apply it to their daily lives. But we cannot know Him—*really* know Him, as in a relationship—unless we become like Him. That will hurt. It does painful damage to our sinful nature to become holy. We are slow to let it go.

Have you assumed that God would never ask you to forsake some of your natural tendencies? Don't. He certainly will. That sin you tolerate? Let it go. However painful it is, let Him rework you. Abandon all that isn't just like His pure, perfect character. Be holy.

To love Jesus is to love holiness.
DAVID SMITHERS

Humble Deeds

Who is wise and understanding
among you? Let them show it by
their good life, by deeds done in the
humility that comes from wisdom.

JAMES 3:13

Hope In The Word

If Proverbs is the wisdom book of the Old
Testament, James is the wisdom book of the New.
There, the profound theology of the early church is
applied. Real faith is demonstrated and good works
are the result. The truth of the gospel comes to life
for the poor, the widows, the tongues of the saints,

the suffering church, and the faithful who pray. And, according to James, it is all characterized by humility.

Why is humility a natural by-product of wisdom? Because wisdom knows who God is and it knows who we are. It sees the remarkable contrast between the two and accepts that God has saved us anyway. It acknowledges the utter depravity of the human condition, but affirms the glory of redemption. Where can pride fit into such an understanding? It can't. Wisdom rules it out. Humility grows in those who see things as they really are.

When we find pride in the church, we can be sure there are believers there who don't really understand the gospel. Pride can never exist where the gospel is clearly understood. The fact that we all struggle with pride doesn't alter that truth at all; we all struggle with the depth and the majesty of the gospel as well. It takes a lifetime to really sink in.

Hope In Deed

Ask yourself a probing question. Do your good works result in pride or in humility? If in pride, then you are doing them to earn favor from God. That is not the gospel, it is legalism. If in humility, then you are doing them because of the amazing grace you've experienced.

Be extremely wary of pride, but do not mistake it for satisfaction. The wise and understanding life of which James speaks is deeply satisfying, but it is not proud. How can it be? The good news of the mercy of God precludes it. Grace removes all sense of worthiness. We do our deeds in humility because we have no other reason to do them.

**He who knows himself best
esteems himself least.**
HENRY G. BROWN

Peace

Let the peace of Christ rule in your hearts.
COLOSSIANS 3:15

Hope In The Word

Peace is elusive. Not only is it elusive to governments in the world's hot spots of conflict, it is elusive in public and private institutions. Unfortunately, it is also elusive in churches and families. And, most unsettling to us, it is elusive in our own hearts.

Ever since the Garden of Eden, the human

heart is by nature unsettled. We are restless creatures because we have separated ourselves from our created purpose. The natural dependence our first parents felt for God has been lost on us. Insecurity reigns within; and where insecurity reigns, peace doesn't.

The reason we live in a world that is in conflict is because we have hearts in conflict. We want to institute the rule of Christ in our hearts, but He must replace the reign of self—with all its fears, ambitions, passions, and false hopes—and that takes time. Human beings in such turmoil find it difficult to live in peace with others, whether it is on the job, in the church, or at home. Those who do not get along with others are invariably uncomfortable with themselves. Those who are at peace within are almost always at peace with others. Even when others rage against them—as they did with Jesus on the cross, Stephen before the Sanhedrin, and Paul from city to city—they do nothing to fuel the conflict. They have no need. They are at peace with themselves and at peace with God.

Hope In Deed

Paul says we are to let the peace of Christ rule in our hearts. He doesn't say peace is simply to exist in our hearts. He doesn't say it is to influence our hearts periodically. It is to rule.

Take this diagnostic test: Are you in conflict with others? It is likely a reflection of the condition of your heart. Ask God to still your turbulent waters. Let Jesus rule in the deepest corners of your being. Know the depths of His peace.

You have made us for Yourself,
and our hearts are restless till
they find their rest in You.
ST. AUGUSTINE

Wisdom in Community

The way of fools seems right to them,
but the wise listen to advice.
PROVERBS 12:15

Hope In The Word

How do the wise know their decisions are sound?
How do fools know theirs are not? Neither question can be answered by looking within. The human
heart is not reliable in matters of wisdom. We hope
our perspectives are based on reality, but there are
always distortions, always perceptual filters through

which we receive our information. The way that seems right to us may—or may not—be right.

The history of Israel is filled with two contrasting approaches to life. In Deuteronomy, God and Moses repeatedly urge the people to do what is right in the eyes of the Lord. In Judges, everyone did what was right in his or her own eyes. Thereafter, Scripture clearly points out that godly kings did right in God's eyes. Ungodly kings did right in their own eyes. But nearly all thought they were doing right.

Our period of history is one in which most people do right in their own eyes. Ethics are considered by most to be relative. People live as ships with no anchor. Each has his own god. We are urged by popular spiritual leaders to look within for the answers, for deep in the human heart we will find our true calling and follow our course. Nothing could be more unbiblical. Fools aren't aware of their foolishness. How can we know what is right? By feeling? By following momentary or self-derived desires? Is there any objective standard by which wisdom is measured?

Hope In Deed

There is, of course. The Bible gives us solid wisdom on which to base our lives. But while it is absolute, its interpretation can vary widely. That's where advice comes in. Never underestimate the body of Christ. He has crafted us to live in community. Wisdom usually comes not to godly individuals but to godly fellowships.

Are you seeking direction? Know your heart, but do not trust it entirely. Measure it by biblical wisdom and the counsel of those who follow it well.

**Seek the advice of your betters
in preference to following
your own inclinations.**
THOMAS À KEMPIS

The Word of Delight

Oh, how I love your law!
I meditate on it all day long.
PSALM 119:97

Hope In The Word

Even when we are convinced of the necessity of
reading our Bible daily and applying its truths, we
can get bogged down in the obligation of doing
so. Somehow, perhaps not coincidentally, when we
determine to learn Scripture with an open heart, the
rest of life seems to close in around it. Schedules get

more complicated, demands get more intense, pressing needs seem to preclude our time of meditation. Our enemy makes sure of it, and God allows him to—it's a test of our devotion to the Word of Life.

But even when we stick with it, there are times of delight and times of passive indifference. It's human nature. What thrills us one day can often bore us the next, even when the subject is something as substantial as God's Word.

What are we to do? How can we maintain our delight in the Bible? Perhaps it is a matter of perspective. We can easily come to view the Scriptures as irrelevant relics of a different age—one that has little consistency with an era of global multiculturalism and technological marvels. We need to remember that the human heart and its relationships are essentially the same as they were thousands of years ago—steeped in self and sin and prone to conflict and dissatisfaction.

Hope In Deed

If you see the Bible as a collection of ancient writings, it might impress you, but it will not change your life very much. If, however, you see it as the vessel that holds the deep mysteries of God, the key that opens life's secret ways, it will have amazing transforming power. The Word of God could do no less—it breathes life into dead souls and causes all that was stale and stagnant within us to flourish.

When the Bible becomes boring to you, perhaps it's because you have reached a spiritual plateau on your journey into God's heart. Ask Him to take you deeper. It is hard to imagine any good father who would reject such a request from his child—least of all ours.

The Bible is a window in this prison-world, through which we may look into eternity.
TIMOTHY DWIGHT

Constant Change

There is a time for everything,
and a season for every activity
under the heavens.
ECCLESIASTES 3:1

Hope In The Word

The human experience is filled with anticipation
of the good things and dread of the bad. We have
dreams, goals, hidden desires, and needful impulses.
When we most expect fruit and fulfillment, we find
none. Often when we expect barrenness, God gives
fruit. The seasons of life frustrate us.

The writer of Ecclesiastes—Solomon, most likely—is aged and philosophical, and while he does not embody the hope that Christians have been given, he knows a thing or two about finite life in this physical world. He has seen emptiness and futility. And, apart from God, he has seen meaninglessness. If there is no God, if no afterlife, if no hidden hope that we cannot see, then there's no point to any of this life that we're living. And still, blind to a discernible purpose, Solomon is able to say: "There is a time for everything."

Solomon has seen seasons come and go. He knows the cyclical pattern of living is not just a matter for meteorologists, it's also a matter for relationships, labor, and the myriad emotions we have. In our lives, there *will* be unfruitful seasons. There *will* be times of discouragement and even despair. There *will* be pointless tasks and intractable conflict. Interspersed with all the joys of the human experience, there will be latent seasons, periods of fallow ground and backward regress. It won't be all good, all the time.

Hope In Deed

That's important for us to know. We'll drive ourselves crazy if we don't understand that there are seasons in our lives. If you're particularly fruitless now—or even fruitful—know that it's only for a time. If a relationship is difficult—or even perfect—it, too, is only for a time. We have to get used to constant change.

Many Christians kick themselves or question God when life isn't running smoothly. Don't. It's only for a season. Do not expect your entire year to be warm and sunny. Part of it will be cold and rainy. And if you're in winter now, know that spring is on the way. Its time always comes.

After winter comes the summer. After night comes the dawn. And after every storm, there come clear, open skies.
SAMUEL RUTHERFORD

Constant Need

Elijah was afraid and ran for his life.
1 KINGS 19:3

Hope In The Word

James was right when he wrote that "Elijah was a human being, even as we are" (James 5:17). Though most of us don't have a ministry the magnitude of Elijah's, we have a fear reflex equal to his. Elijah had spent the last few days proving the power of God over the empty religion of Baal. He had been viewing eternal truth with his very human eyes. Suddenly, when Jezebel sought his life, he viewed his circumstances through those same lenses, but with unexpected fear. This time, those eyes didn't see the glory of God, only the wrath of Jezebel. He was afraid—just like us.

What is it about us that can see eternal majesties at inspired moments and then can cower at ungodly threats at other moments? Does the Holy Spirit come and go that freely from our hearts? Perhaps it's just that we are so thoroughly infused with human frailty that we can only get glimpses of divine power. Perhaps we are simply inconsistent in our devotion. Perhaps faith is a muscle that is sometimes, for some reason, reluctant to work. Though faith is, in a sense, our resting in God, we can still get tired. We pass seamlessly from anxiety to divine glory to anxiety again, hardly ever realizing what empowers us one day and not another.

A heart of wisdom will come to grips with such human inconsistencies. We must settle in our own minds the fact that we are never self-sufficient and always dependent. Great successes do not eliminate deep needs; it's a fact of the human condition. We have to get used to it.

Hope In Deed

We must battle constantly against two relentless urges: the urge to think great victories should be followed by self-sufficiency; and the urge to let visible circumstances rule our thinking. Elijah, the great prophet of Israel, gave in to both. So do we. Frequently.

Never let the visible rule. Your victory yesterday does not decide your status today. Neither do your enemies. You need God desperately every day equally, regardless of how threatening—or how successful—things look.

O God, never suffer us to think that we can stand by ourselves, and not need Thee.
JOHN DONNE

Measured Words

Do not be quick with your mouth,
do not be hasty in your heart to
utter anything before God.
ECCLESIASTES 5:2

Hope In The Word

If you had an appointment to confer with the president in the Oval Office, would you prepare? Would you plan what you were going to say before you saw him, or would you just play it by ear? All but the most reckless and careless of us would consider our words wisely. We'd realize we're meeting with someone who has the power to change things. We'd think about what we want changed.

But we rarely approach God that way. Perhaps it's our awareness that our time with Him is unlimited. Perhaps we've heard so many pastors and teachers tell us that even our smallest concerns are His concerns. Perhaps we've interpreted His generous time and detailed care as reasons that prayer can be casual. If so, we've misunderstood. God does give us unlimited time, and He does care about the details. But prayer is anything but casual.

Jesus rebuked both religious hypocrites and pagans for their many words. Maybe He was zeroing in on their annoying repetitions, but He also pointed out their false idea that many words get God's ear (Matthew 6:7). He also warned that we will be accountable for every careless word we've spoken (Matthew 12:36). And we can assume that His standards for prayer are probably not lower than His standards for conversation.

Hope In Deed

God encourages us to come to His throne with boldness and confidence (Hebrews 4:16). But He does not encourage us to come to His throne with carelessness. Our words in prayer carry incredible weight. They should be well considered.

Perhaps a good approach to prayer would be to take Solomon's advice. After all, God surely has more important information to share with us than we have to share with Him. Yes, He wants to hear our desires. He also wants us to listen to His. Both are extremely important.

When you pray, rather let your heart be without words than your words be without heart.
JOHN BUNYAN

The Highest Standard

It is the Father, living in me,
who is doing his work.
JOHN 14:10

Hope In The Word

Christians commonly take one of two approaches to
a verse like this. The first approach is assuming that
because Jesus was God incarnate, His relationship
to the Father was unique and exclusive to Him. A
logical conclusion, following that assumption, is that
Jesus is the only One who can ever say these words

about the Father doing His work in Him. With this understanding, we may marvel at Jesus' identity, but we can never participate in it.

The second approach assumes that the relationship Jesus had with the Father—while unique in the sense that He is the only begotten Son of God—is nevertheless an example for us to follow. If so, He demonstrates the full potential of a human being completely surrendered to God and immersed in His will. With that understanding, we not only marvel at Jesus' identity, we can participate in it.

Which of these approaches should we take? Is Jesus one of a kind in His relationship with the Father? Or does He offer that relationship to us? The rest of the New Testament makes it clear. If we are obedient and request this amazing relationship, we can quote these words of Jesus for ourselves: "It is the Father, living in me, who is doing his work."

Is it presumptuous to say such a thing? Paul did. See Galatians 2:20 and all the other verses in which he refers to Christ living in him. The Scriptures scream this truth at us, from Jesus' declaration a few verses later about doing His work (John 14:12), to Pentecost, to Revelation. It is implied everywhere. Jesus is not just our Savior; He is our life.

Hope In Deed

Do you see Jesus' life and works as an impossibly high standard? They are, if we rely on our human capabilities. But Jesus offers His Spirit to live within us. Accept Him. Rely on Him. Ask for a greater display of His life within you. Do not settle for less. Our knowledge of His presence and strength within us makes all the difference.

No man can do the work of God
until he has the Holy Spirit and
is endued with power.
GEORGE CAMPBELL MORGAN

Day 27

Numbered Days

Teach us to number our days, that
we may gain a heart of wisdom.
PSALM 90:12

Hope In The Word

Against all evidence to the contrary, we grow up
thinking we are invincible. There is something deep
in the human soul—something placed there by the
God who created us for eternity—that tells us life
is endless. It is, but there is a substantial difference
between the life we live now and the life we live in

eternity. They overlap, but in only one can we bear fruit for the other. What we do today can have everlasting consequences. We can invest in the treasures of the Kingdom of God.

So many lives end in regret over this revelation. Many of us let our days pass by in survival mode or in entertainment mode, never balancing such concerns with the eternal fruits that matter more. We are to plant so that our God may reap and reward. And in order to sow effectively, we must sow with a clear awareness that the time to plant is extremely short. The window of opportunity for fruit bearing is narrow indeed.

James tells us our life is a vapor. David agrees: "Everyone is but a breath" (Psalm 39:5). In the grand, eternal scheme of things, we are a small point on the timeline. By the time we learn what we need to know and are equipped to serve, we have but a moment left. But God has given us an awesome privilege. We can accomplish in that moment works of such significance that they will last forever. God can change people's lives through us. He can shape our children and our spouses and our friends through us. He can feed the hungry, encourage the outcast, redeem the lost, heal the sick, cultivate worshipers, and build His Kingdom through us. But only if we're wise and have numbered our days.

Hope In Deed

Paul tells us to redeem the time because the days are evil (Ephesians 5:16, KJV). They are fleeting days, slipping by us before we've hardly noticed. We must number them. We must live with an eye on the limitations of time and the certainty of death. Wisdom fills the hearts of those who can live with such perspective.

Time is given us to use in view of eternity.
ANONYMOUS

The Merciful

I knew that you are a gracious and
compassionate God, slow to anger
and abounding in love, a God who
relents from sending calamity.

JONAH 4:2

Hope In The Word

One of the more colorful examples of the need for
mercy in the Old Testament is a negative example:
Jonah. He knew that God was a compassionate God,
and he did not want God to show compassion to the
Ninevites. So he disobeyed. When he was compelled
to obey, he complained. Somehow, the compassion

of God did not translate into the compassion of Jonah.

Do we find ourselves in such a predicament? Having been abundantly blessed with God's mercy—the unmerited grace and forgiveness we've received for our rebellion against the Most High—do we then stand in judgment of others? The idea is ludicrous, but nearly all of us are guilty. Jesus has a Beatitude He'd like us to hear: "Blessed are the merciful, for they will be shown mercy" (Matthew 5:7). The implication is sobering: Those who are not merciful will not be shown mercy. That has to hurt. We know it has applied, at least in some degree, to each of us.

Those who have not shown mercy have never understood God's. They just don't get it. They don't understand the depths from which we've been saved and the relative pettiness with which we judge others. They still think an attainable righteousness is the key, and they compel others to strive for it.

Hope In Deed

Have you ever found yourself passing judgment on someone else and then remembering the guilt that we have all shared before God? That is the prompting of the Holy Spirit, reminding us that we, too, are worthy of judgment and unworthy of mercy. Let the reminder sink in. God overflows with compassion for those who are lost and sinful, and if we are to be like Him at all, we must share that compassion. We must understand mercy.

Do you wish to receive mercy?
Show mercy to your neighbor.
JOHN CHRYSOSTOM

A Certain Providence

LORD, you alone are my portion and
my cup; you make my lot secure.
PSALM 16:5

Hope In The Word

Many foolish decisions have been made out of the
emptiness of discontentment. That's a frightening
place from which to guide a life, but we do it often.
We want something more, something better, because
we're not quite happy with our lot in life. We forget
one unwavering scriptural principle: God is the
Author of our lot.

There's nothing wrong with a holy ambition. The key for us is to make sure it's actually holy. God has placed within us a desire to work and to accomplish things, especially for His glory. But we can deceive ourselves easily, thinking that we're working for God when in fact we're working to escape the place He's put us. Contentment is the fruit of godly wisdom and a wonderful attitude to hold, and it begins with the certain knowledge of this verse: "LORD, you alone are my portion."

We do not live in a content culture. Our society is moved primarily by restlessness. Deep down we know that things aren't right, and the knee-jerk reaction of a secular world is to try to fix the situation. We who are in Christ know better: He is the Fixer, and only our trust in Him will deliver us from our restlessness. That trust, if cultivated rightly, will give us the contentment that David expresses in this psalm. It will define for us our security.

Hope In Deed

Did David write of his peace while he was sitting on a throne or hiding in a cave? Was he dancing in praise or grieving his son Absalom? It doesn't matter. The key to contentment is to refuse to define your life by your present circumstances. It is to know that you are where you are because God is sovereign. Even when the situation is desperate, we can say that "the boundary lines have fallen for me in pleasant places" (Psalm 16:6). Why? Because we've been given a glimpse of the end of the story and the One who guides it. Whatever we're going through, it will end well if we trust Him. Faith believes that truth, clings to it, and thrives on it. The result is the wisdom of contentment.

If we do not have quiet in our minds,
outward comfort will do no more for us
than a golden slipper on a gouty foot.
JOHN BUNYAN

Day 30

Know Your Roots

The righteous will flourish like a
palm tree . . . ; planted in the house
of the LORD, they will flourish
in the courts of our God.

PSALM 92:12-13

Hope In The Word

The shifting sands of this world are fertile ground
for nothing but fear. We see uncertainty all around
us—in stock markets, in the comings and goings
of military forces, in rapidly spreading pathogens,
in red alerts and brown skies. We can easily panic
under the illusion this world presents to us: that we
are in a very fragile place where nothing is sure.

But that's not the place God provides for His people. Yes, this age, with all its chaos, can be frightening at first glance. That's why we cannot settle for first glance. We must look deeper, to the One who gives us promises of refuge and strength. He is our tower, our fortress, and our help, as so many of the psalms tell us. And in Psalm 92, He gives us a promise: "The righteous will flourish."

That's great news except for one unsettling fact: Deep down inside, we question our righteousness. We know we've earned nothing before God. So how can this passage encourage us? We know the Righteous One. *He* will flourish, and we are in Him. The Bible is very emphatic about that, and we can take it literally. In Jesus, we exist. His death was ours, His resurrection is ours, and His life at the right hand of the Father is ours (Ephesians 2:6; Colossians 3:1). He lives in us, and we live in Him. It's an unalterable, blessed fact.

Hope In Deed

What does that mean for our fear? It means that when the towers of this world collapse, we stand firm. It means that when the bombs of this world explode, we keep it together. It all depends on where we're rooted.

Do you feel rooted in shifting sand, vulnerable to the scarecrow tactics of a panicked society? Reconsider your position in Christ. Those rooted in the world will shake when the world shakes. Those rooted in Jesus will never shake when the world shakes, because when the world shakes, Jesus stands unmoved. Cling to Him. Trust Him. Remember that you live where He lives.

On Christ the solid Rock I stand;
all other ground is sinking sand.
EDWARD MOTE

Wisdom Waits

The LORD rewards everyone for their
righteousness and faithfulness.

1 SAMUEL 26:23

Hope In The Word

David had the opportunity that every oppressed,
abused person dreams of: a chance to rid himself
of his archenemy. As Saul lay sleeping in his camp,
David sneaked through the ranks and put himself
in position to thrust a spear into his rival. Surely
he hadn't risked so much entering this camp just to
prove a point. But, in fact, he had. As in a similar

golden opportunity weeks before, he had no intention of laying a hand on "the LORD's anointed" (1 Samuel 26:9). David remembered what most of us forget: Our times are in God's hands.

Most of us would have thought as David's companion did. Abishai interpreted the event as God's provision, an ordained moment to throw off the yoke of an oppressive, mad king. Surely God had put David in this strategic position for a reason! And He had; but Abishai thought the reason was Saul's demise. David knew the reason was to make a statement about his intentions, his innocence, and God's sovereignty. He had not forgotten that God had placed Saul in his kingship. He dared not violate God's anointing—even when it had been abused.

Such sensitivity to the wisdom of God would serve us well. David knew Saul would die in God's timing; but he wasn't convinced that he himself was an instrument of God's timing. So he restrained himself. When it comes to God's will, assertiveness is only appropriate when the path is certain. This path wasn't certain. Restraint was the better part of faith.

Hope In Deed

How do you approach God's will? When God's direction seems probable to you, do you forge ahead? Don't. God never asks us to move ahead on the basis of probabilities. He commands us to move ahead on the basis of His certain promises. But our actions should never be more definite than His timing. If His plan isn't clear, it is not time to move forward. God does *not* help those who help themselves. He helps those who trust His sovereignty. He honors faithfulness. When God's plan is unclear, wisdom waits.

**God aims to exalt Himself by working
for those who wait for Him.**
JOHN PIPER

History Lessons

They forgot what he had done, the
wonders he had shown them.

PSALM 78:11

Hope In The Word

God has done great things. Many of them are
recorded in the written Word by generations who
wanted their descendants to know of His faithfulness. Many of them are the subjects of biographies
and church traditions. But many of them are relics
of history, forgotten by a forgetful humanity. They

are often buried in the minds of those who have passed on. Sometimes they are faint hints in our subconscious that God has done something good for us, but we can't remember what. The wonders were marvelous at the time, but they are wasted in the present. Far too often, we don't let the lingering goodness of God linger long enough.

Why not? What is it about us that can remember who insulted us decades ago but cannot remember the deliverance God gave us last year? We can hold a grudge for a lifetime, but when asked how God has answered our prayers in the past, we struggle for a response. It's not that He hasn't answered our prayers, even dramatically sometimes. No, the problem is that we are always focused on the next hurdle, the next problem, the next goal. God is only relevant in our minds when He is relevant to today's needs.

He would actually seem more relevant to today's needs if we could rehearse and remember His past victories. It's much easier to pray to the God who delivered us from an impossible situation when we remember the deliverance. We pray with faith when His miraculous strength stands out in our minds. We pray with ambiguity and doubt when it doesn't.

Hope In Deed

Make sure His strength stands out in your mind. If you are not in the practice of keeping a prayer log, begin the practice now. It doesn't need to be elaborate. Just make a list of what you ask God for, and then when He answers, check it off. Then in a day of distress, review all the checks—and watch your faith grow. The spiritual markers you put up in your life will largely determine the depth of your faith today.

When remembrance of God lives in
the heart . . . then all goes well.

THEOPHAN THE RECLUSE

Confidence in God

**Though war break out against me,
even then I will be confident.**
PSALM 27:3

Hope In The Word

Feeling besieged? Don't be surprised. It's a natural human condition. Few people go through life with a sense of invulnerability. We question our strength, and, when trouble strikes, we doubt our ability to stand. We don't feel invincible, so we fear trials. When war or even minor conflicts break out against us, confidence often disappears.

David was no stranger to conflict. He was also no stranger to fear. His understanding of God's strength and sovereignty did not come by birthright; it came by experience. When he tells us in Psalm 27:1 that the Lord is his light and salvation, the stronghold of his life, he can make such claims only because there were times when he was forced either to lean on God or to wither away and die. The truth of God's strength is learned only during times of vulnerability. Strong, confident people learn to rely on themselves. Weak, helpless people learn to rely on God.

David's introductory question in this psalm—"whom shall I fear?"—is purely rhetorical. He knows the answer: no one. If we can honestly claim with David that the Lord is our light, salvation, and stronghold, we can ask the same question without any fear of a valid answer coming up. We can be afraid of no one.

Hope In Deed

If you're trying to work yourself into a state of confidence, be careful of where that confidence is placed. The model of overassertive strength that the world urges us to follow overestimates the power of man. Christians are not called to follow it; we are called to place every hope in the almighty God. If we need a source of strength, our inner self will not encourage us very much. God will.

Learn to speak the words of David. Say them out loud to yourself, if necessary. You are not playing psychological games; you are rehearsing the truth. Though war break out against us, we have every indication that our confidence in God is well-founded. Our heart does not need to fear, because we are children of the fearless One.

Confidence in the natural world
is self-reliance; in the spiritual
world it is God-reliance.
OSWALD CHAMBERS

Peace Like a River

If only you had paid attention to
my commands, your peace would
have been like a river, your well-
being like the waves of the sea.
ISAIAH 48:18

Hope In The Word

If only. Those two words are small in their grammat-
ical placement but enormous in their tragic implications. They mean that things could have been
different. Much different. They mean that if the
response of God's people had been other than it was,
much heartache could have been avoided. Blessing
would have flowed, but it didn't. If only.

Like Isaiah, we've spoken them too. Everyone has regrets. That's part of living in a fallen world. We know if we had been more diligent and faithful, our lives today could be radically different than they turned out. Even if we're happy right now, we wonder what could have been and what would have been. Why? Because sooner or later we come to a melancholy realization: Life can always be better.

We seek the God of comfort to tell us why bad things have happened—why we're in debt, why we lost that job, why our family isn't a happy one, why our dreams aren't fulfilled. But deep down we know. It isn't because God let us down; it's because we let Him down. We didn't live up to His instructions. That dreaded rebellious streak that we all seem to have has led us in futile directions contrary to the explicit teaching of our Maker. We don't know what we were thinking when we went away from Him, but we want to come back. His plan is better; we know that now. We want to be restored to a place of peace like a river and righteousness like the sea.

Hope In Deed

That's the beauty of the gospel of grace. It never puts us in an unredeemable position. Whenever we say, "If only," God says, "Now you can." Maybe there are lost years, but they are past. God can redeem them for a bountiful future. The important thing is that we've learned that His voice is not demanding for His own ego but insistent for our own good. We can follow Him with trust that His way leads to peace and righteousness. We *must* follow Him with that trust. If we can, we'll be blessed. If only.

Stayed upon Jehovah, hearts
are fully blessed, finding, as He
promised, perfect peace and rest.
FRANCES RIDLEY HAVERGAL

Choices

**The way of the sluggard is blocked
with thorns, but the path of
the upright is a highway.**
PROVERBS 15:19

Hope In The Word

Every single moment of our lives, we face a choice.
We choose when to speak and when to keep silent,
when to sit and when to stand, when to breathe and
when to hold our breath. We could get incredibly
detailed about all of our many momentary options
if we wanted to. But that's an excruciating exercise,

sort of like listening to every beat of our heart. It requires too much attention and stress. We prefer to let things happen naturally and automatically.

But Proverbs urges us to step back and look at our choices from time to time—not just the major ones, but also the little ones that determine the subtle directions of our lives each day. And its message is consistent: Righteous choices, while sometimes harder in the short term, are always easier in the long run. They lead to life. Laziness and evil put us on hard roads. The path of least resistance is often the path of greatest grief.

That doesn't mean that righteous choices will always make things easy for us. Anytime we seek to obey God diligently and serve Him with devotion, there will be obstacles. But God always paves a way for our path of discipleship. He doesn't ever make rebellion or laziness profitable in the end.

Hope In Deed

What level of diligence guides your life? Are you proactive about your choices—even the small ones—or are you herded like livestock through the fields of life, unwittingly pushed and pulled by those around you? Do you feel that God is firmly directing your steps? Or do you feel that you're just floating with the current and conforming to the expectations of this world?

God calls for diligence. Laziness and discipleship do not mix. He doesn't mean for us to obsess about every minor choice, but He expects us to draw a line in the sand and refuse to let the demands of the culture dictate our lives. We are to guard His plan for our lives with zeal. Don't get off the highway. Let Him be Lord of your choices.

Every day the choice between good and
evil is presented to us in simple ways.
WILLIAM SANGSTER

The Real Thing

Love must be sincere.
ROMANS 12:9

Hope In The Word

We are called by Jesus to love one another. Love is the defining characteristic of the Christian community; Jesus called it His "new command" and said it would distinguish us as His disciples (John 13:34-35). He did not lay it out for us as a good option; it was an order. Obedience requires that we love Him and that we love others.

Knowing that, we usually try to put on love—or at least the appearance of love. Even when we cultivate bitterness in our hearts toward another, we cultivate smiles and warmth on our faces. Our words and our inner feelings do not always match. We act loving because we know we are supposed to; but we do not *feel* loving. That's a problem.

Which is genuine love? When Paul tells us to love each other sincerely, does he really expect our feelings to fall in line with our obedience? Is it acceptable to *act* loving rather than to *be* loving? It's a start, but we can't be content with that. Our feelings change slowly, especially when we've been offended or slighted. In such cases, we can at least act as we know we are supposed to act. But we cannot stop there. We must guard our hearts diligently. That is where all actions will eventually flow from. At some point, obedience must include sincerity. Otherwise, it doesn't come close to the character of God.

Think about that. Does God love us reluctantly? Does He say: "You've sinned so much that I don't have strong feelings for you, but according to My promise I'll treat you lovingly"? Of course not. There is no internal contradiction in God's attitudes. He is not superficial in the least. His love is real—the most authentic, genuine love there is. So must ours be.

Hope In Deed

How can we get there? Genuine love is so hard,
especially when we're told to love our enemies!
Fallen, sinful natures cannot fulfill that command.
The answer must be supernatural.

Trust God to live His life in you. That's what
our life in the Holy Spirit is all about. Ask Him not
to reform your character by giving you love, but to
replace your character by giving you His. His love is
utterly sincere. Ours must be as well.

Has God commanded something? Then
throw yourself back on God for the
means to do what He has commanded.
WATCHMAN NEE

A New Culture

Hate what is evil;
cling to what is good.
ROMANS 12:9

Hope In The Word

A man went to live in a foreign country. He loved it.
He wanted to apply for citizenship, and having no
real ties to his former country, he began to live "like
the natives." He adopted the dress and habits of his
new culture. He began to learn the language. He
refused to eat food from his former diet and dined

exclusively on the cuisine of his adopted homeland. He wanted no visual reminders of his past and embraced all the customs of his present and future. He established a new identity.

That's what God tells us to do. We have left the kingdom of darkness and been adopted into the Kingdom of light. We are to put off the clothing of the old nature and live in the Spirit of the new. We are conforming to a different culture and being shaped into a different nature. The old has passed away; all things have become new.

When Paul tells us to hate what is evil and cling to what is good, he is not giving us friendly advice. He is using graphic images to define our transition. We are to "turn in horror from wickedness" (Romans 12:9, AMPC), loathing any semblance of ungodliness. The deeds of darkness are no longer appropriate in our new Kingdom; they do not fit into this culture. And then we are to cling to what is good—embrace it, desperately grab hold of it, never let it go. It is to be our obsession, of a sort. We are to pursue godliness with unbridled zeal.

Hope In Deed
Few Christians make such a dramatic transition, but those who do can testify to the rest of us that

it's a greater blessing to make radical changes than to make slow, imperceptible ones. Sanctification is a lifelong process, but blessed are those who are on the fast track. They are quicker candidates for usefulness in the Kingdom, they are greater testimonies to the power of God, and they are less likely to fade away into the apostasy of lukewarmness. Real godliness is radical.

Are you in a spiritual rut? Hate what is evil and cling to what is good. Let sin horrify you, and embrace the culture of the Kingdom of blazing light. Total immersion is always the best way to fit in.

He that sees the beauty of
holiness . . . sees the greatest and
most important thing in the world.
JONATHAN EDWARDS

Purpose in Planning

The plans of the diligent lead to profit
as surely as haste leads to poverty.
PROVERBS 21:5

Hope In The Word

"Haste makes waste." It's a proverb many of us grew up with, and it's a reflection of biblical truth. Those who are diligent and want to accomplish much cannot approach life haphazardly. Diligence implies a plan, and haste is an enemy of planning.

We who are remade in God's image can take our

cues from God. The Bible frequently refers to His plans, and we often refer to the plan of salvation, the plan for the end times, and all sorts of other designs from His hand. We can be reasonably sure that God didn't figure out what to do on the second day of creation after He got through with the first. His wisdom had a purpose in mind when He began. And His plans have been long and thorough. God does not make it up on the run. Neither should we.

God is certainly not an enemy of spontaneity, but He is an enemy of carelessness. Philip was responding spontaneously when God put him on the Gaza road; Peter was flexible when God told him to go to Cornelius; and Paul was able to turn from Asia to Macedonia when God redirected him. Those of us who make plans and will not diverge from them under any circumstances have deified the plans. We must always hold God above them, not them above God. But given His authority, we are urged to live wisely in this world. And wisdom calls for the intentional pursuit of a godly purpose.

Hope In Deed

Consider the stewardship of your time. Is it spent efficiently? Don't think that God wants us working as machines and suppressing individuality.

And don't think that He discourages us from being flexible and available when He directs us. But also don't assume that He advocates a random approach to our lives. The God with a purpose bears children with a purpose. And the God who has a plan to accomplish His purposes bears children who will also plan to accomplish His purposes. Without a goal, we are aimless—even when we're incredibly busy. God calls us to aim high and to know how to get there.

Purpose is what gives life a meaning. . . .
A drifting boat always drifts downstream.
CHARLES H. PARKHURST

Who You Are

You are the salt of the earth. . . .
You are the light of the world.
MATTHEW 5:13-14

Hope In The Word

Jesus has gathered an odd collection of disciples and
other listeners to a place on a hillside. His opening
words to them are perhaps a little surprising. The
way to blessedness, He has told them, is through
poverty, grief, meekness, hunger and thirst, mercy,
purity, pacifism, and persecution. These aren't the

standards human beings are prone to strive for. Nevertheless, they are the divine prescription for a fallen character.

His next statements are a little more promising, however. "You are the salt of the earth," He tells them; and not only that, they are "the light of the world." That's a little more affirming, a positive statement that is sure to stroke the self-importance of the listeners. But Jesus' statements about our identity are more than positive affirmation; they are an indication of our responsibility. Those who follow Him have taken on the weight of influencing the grave situation that this world finds itself in.

The principle is that God's people are key to the Kingdom of God in this world. That Kingdom is coming, but not apart from the work of its ambassadors. Those who hear Jesus, who have ears to hear truth and act on it, are the vehicle of God's activity in this world. They are salt and light, preserving, seasoning, illuminating, and pointing to the one true Light. There is something profound and humbling about a God who does His work through a ragtag collection of redeemed throwaways. The scavenger God has gathered a remnant for an amazing re-genesis through the coming of His Son.

Hope In Deed

Our lives are largely shaped by our perceptions of ourselves. Perhaps that's why Satan has targeted our sense of identity from Eden until now. So Jesus begins His great sermon with words designed to bring our self-perception in line with His truth. We can never come to grips with reality—God's reality—until we understand His assessment of ourselves and begin to live accordingly: We are called to be His salt and His light in a decaying, dark world.

According to the New Testament,
God wills that the church be a people
who show what God is like.
STANLEY J. GRENZ

Celebrate Good Times

When times are good, be happy.
ECCLESIASTES 7:14

Hope In The Word

Some Christians feel guilty when they are happy. With a personal history of sin, a world of grief, and so much to be done before Jesus returns, how can times be good? They look at the heart of God and see only sadness and stress. They reason that a good God could not be happy with what He sees and, therefore, neither can we.

But God has not created us for futility. This is perhaps a surprising message from the sad book of Ecclesiastes, but we read about this God of joy in other books of the Bible too. Fruitfulness, prosperity, blessedness, contentment, and inner peace are all gifts from above. And it's never wrong to enjoy His gifts.

Is that hard to do? Some people have too easy a time of it, but historically some of our denominations and theological perspectives have discouraged happiness. They meant to discourage meaningless and profane frivolity, not true joy. The Christian life is to be a joyful life; the Bible makes that clear. Rather than always seeing what's wrong in our lives, what's wrong in the world, and what God wants to do to fill in the gaps, we are to frequently look at what God has given us, how He has blessed His gifts, and what He has already done to fill in the gaps. Spiritually speaking, we often barely notice that our glass is filling up; we focus on its remaining emptiness. In truth, we're allowed and even urged to notice that the glass is often half empty on this planet. But we are to dwell on the fact that it's half full.

Thankfulness is to dominate over discontentment in our thinking.

Hope In Deed

How can we do this? Like soldiers in combat, we can be altogether serious about our jobs while still enjoying a rest and a laugh in between the battles. Like athletes in training, we can enjoy the competition now and can already look forward to the victory celebration. If we think being serious about the Kingdom of God means deferring gratification until heaven, we're wrong. God and His gifts are to be enjoyed. Now. When times are good—and if you look hard enough, they usually are—be happy.

Christians are the only people in the world who have anything to be happy about.
BILLY GRAHAM

Walk Thru the Bible

Walk Thru the Bible ignites passion for God's Word through innovative live events, inspiring biblical resources, and a global impact that changes lives worldwide . . . including yours.

Known for innovative methods and high-quality resources, we serve the whole body of Christ across denominational, cultural, and national lines. We partner with the local church worldwide to fulfill its mission, communicating the truths of God's Word in a way that makes the Bible readily accessible to anyone. Through our strong global network, we are strategically positioned to address the church's greatest need: developing mature, committed, and spiritually reproducing believers.

Our live events and small group curricula are taught in more than 50 languages by more than 80,000 people in more than 130 countries. More than 100 million devotionals have been packaged into daily magazines, books, and other publications that reach over five million people each year.

Wherever you are on your journey, we can help.

Walk Thru the Bible
walkthru.org
1.800.361.6131